# The Newtonian System for Accelerated, Lasting Financial Wealth & Security

## By Greg Gootee

*This Book is Dedicated to Donna.
My Best Friend, My Wife, and My Life*

The Author may be contacted at the following address:

**Greg Gootee**

GregGGootee@gmail.com

# Contents

## Introduction

If you're like most readers, you are probably thinking right now that the name of this book is quite a mouthful. You're right, and I meant it to be a mouthful. I named this book in honor of Sir Isaac Newton, one of the greatest and arguably the

greatest scientist and philosopher who ever lived. Newton and his works changed everything about the understanding of this world and how it works. My book aims to change everything about *your* understanding of the

creation process behind financial wealth and security and how it works. Both life changing, albeit Newton's might have been a little bit farther reaching for civilization at large. I would argue, however, that the information in *this book* can change your life every bit as significantly and substantially as the information in Newton's *Philosophiae Naturalis Principia Mathematica* did for the readers of his day.

Is that a bit grandiose? Possibly, but in the first chapter, I will tell you exactly why I am comfortable making these claims. Furthermore, I will give you demonstrable evidence that the methods, secrets, and abundance of resources I know you already know exist on the internet but may not know how to access not only exist for a privileged few, but exist for *your use* and *will work for you.* It is those powerful methods, the ones I will illuminate in this book, that create life-changing financial wealth and security when leveraged correctly.

## Something Most People Don't Know About Isaac Newton

Most of you reading this probably already know that Isaac Newton is, as I mentioned, one of the greatest scientists and philosophers who ever lived. He discovered plastics, the law of gravity, and the laws of mechanics. He is the creator of calculus. He laid out the three laws of motion, the law of universal gravitation, and the principles of conservation related to momentum and angular momentum. Oh, and he also discovered refraction of light, the empirical law of cooling, and built the first practical telescope. Needless to say, the guy was prolific.

Something most people do not know about Isaac Newton, however, is that he spent half of his life seeking the legendary Philosopher's Stone, a stone capable of transforming base metals like iron into precious metals like gold. Isaac Newton was, to begin with at least, an alchemist, a true originator of the concept of "get rich quick." Sad to say for Newton – but happy for us, since he became an incredible scientist instead – he never found the Philosopher's Stone and he also never figured out how to make one; he never even got near a blueprint. That is because there really would not be a blueprint until centuries later, when this book went into print.

That's right: The information in this book is a clear blueprint to achieving one thing and one thing only. It is a thing we all want and a thing we all need. It is, if we are honest with ourselves, a thing we all *crave* because financial wealth and security, particularly *accelerated financial wealth and security*, allows us to pursue all the other passions, pleasures, and responsibilities we have in our lives with our full attention and dedication. The blueprint could not exist for Newton because the internet did not exist for Newton. Fortunately, it does for you, and you can use the internet as your own personal philosopher's stone to be able to virtually print money on demand – something Newton would have loved, by the way, since he served as Warden of the Royal Mint in London and oversaw production of the pound sterling during his tenure there.

## Let's Get Started.

I don't know when you heard about making money online. I don't know how long you have been thinking about doing it or even trying to do it. What I do know, however, is that time is of the essence.

**Every second you wait is another dollar not in your pocket.**

In the next chapter, I will set the stage for you in terms of what you stand to gain, what you stand to lose, and what you stand to *waste* in terms of literal fortunes lost today that should have been made *overnight, tonight, online.*

You cannot afford to put this book down, so let's get started. Read on.

# Chapter 1: Setting the Stage for Accelerated Financial Wealth & Security

To get us off on the right foot and really set the stage for what is truly possibly using the internet to create meaningful, life-changing income for yourself, your business, and your family, I want to start things off with a little story. It's about that fellow you see in the space above. I like to think of him as an important figure in history – my history at least. I will tell you why he's so important to me today, and then, if you have not already guessed, I will tell you who he is.

Let's get started.

The fellow in the picture above experienced a very serious, life-changing event when he was 42 years old. Prior to that event, he was on top of the world. He had a strong income and had been professionally successful to the extent that he was a senior vice president in a multibillion-dollar company. He was a true expert in his field, sales and marketing, and it seemed to him and the people who knew him that everything was going his way. His client list read like a "Who's Who" list of major corporations, including names we all know like General Electric, IBM, Johnson & Johnson, Johns Hopkins Hospital, Neiman Marcus, Mercedes

Benz, and, well, I think you probably get the picture.

At the age of 42, it seemed like this guy had nothing but blue skies in front of him until those blue skies turned cloudy and everything changed literally overnight. What happened that fateful night? He had a heart attack, and it was not just any old heart attack. It was what is known as a "widow-maker." That kind of heart attack is so severe the chances are very, very high the patient will not survive. Fortunately for my friend, he did survive, but he lost about a third of his heart function in the process. To show you just how serious it was, when he asked the ER doctor if he was going to die, the poor cardiologist had to tell him, "I don't know yet." It was pretty bad.

Thank goodness, the widow-maker did not make this fellow's wife a widow. He made it through. He actually recovered and returned to work, although his entire family was absolutely terrified of losing him and, to make matters harder on his heart, he was the family's primary provider. While his little daughter was wondering aloud if he would be alive to walk her down the aisle, his young son was speculating about whether the family could live under a bridge. The youngest offered to forgo haircuts to save money. It was heart-wrenching, but he made it through. He even went back to work, and for about eight years it seemed like things would mend.

Then, at age 50, it happened again. The second heart attack was just as awful. It was just as severe, and it was far, far more terrifying than the first one because this time, that heart attack came with a catastrophic prognosis: if my friend did not retire permanently and immediately, he would have a third heart attack and the third time around, he most certainly would die. He looked for second opinions, third opinions, fourth ones, but everyone agreed. If he returned to work again, he would quite certainly have another massive heart attack and his chances of survival were near zero. Everything had to change, and it had to change permanently.

Now, at this point in most stories like this one, you would start to hear some very motivational language about appreciating every single day and spending more time with family. I will tell you, this fellow definitely got that. Every day was (and is) certainly a gift. However, put yourself in his shoes for a minute. This is a guy whose kids are still young enough they thought maybe giving up haircuts would solve the financial shortfall left when the family's sole provider went into forced retirement. He has a long way to go supporting his family while never again drawing a salary. It's terrifying. I would add it wasn't very good for his heart, either! He was having to think about things at the age of 50 most people do not even start considering until their 60s, and all he had to tide the family over was some insurance which he knew would eventually run out.

**So, when your options run out, what do you do?**

Being truly out of options is a terrifying position. It's stressful. It's physically and mentally painful. I can tell you *from personal experience* it is very hard on the heart. Yep, that's right: If you hadn't already guessed, that guy in the story is me and his story is my reality.

At age 50, in the prime of my life, at the height of my earnings potential (and that was quite a decent height, I have to emphasize in order to really set the stage correctly moving forward), when everything should have been looking golden for me, my working years were done. They were finished, and there was not a thing I could do about it. If I wanted to continue to support my family, live my life, and get to truly *enjoy* each day the way I knew I should and the way I knew I wanted to, then I had to create income fast.

**That is the truth about what you will ask yourself when your options run out. You will ask yourself, "How can I create income fast?"**

That doesn't make you a bad person. You're not a miser or a Scrooge. You're a leader in your family. You're a support system for your loved ones. You have a burning desire to take care of your family, to create a great life for them in a nice home with a wonderful future. You want to impact the causes that matter most deeply to you, and you are dealing with all of this intense desire while, at the same time, you have had the means to do so, that you were also reliant on, ripped away from you with no warning whatsoever. Let me make this very clear: *There is nothing wrong – and everything right – with asking yourself how to create income fast. Really, really fast.*

And that is why I wanted to set the stage: to show you that I know what it feels like to have a burning desire to support my family and a complete lack of awareness about how I might do it. If you are there right now or even if you are just close, then take heart. When things are very, very bleak, you can have a glimmer of hope. I had that glimmer, and it was not unsubstantial. It was very real, and it was my utter fascination with the internet.

I know. I know. You were hoping for something a little less "mundane." But here's the thing: in this position, you want your hope to be mundane. You don't want a miracle; you want a workable, viable, proven solution. The internet is that, and all you need to have at this very second in order to seize hold of that solution is what I started out with: enough hope to move forward. Keep reading, because everything else you need, I will share with you in the coming chapters.

**"For several years this great man, Isaac Newton, was intensely occupied in endeavoring to discover a way of changing the base metals into gold."**

James Parton, 1868, "Short Lives of the Most Interesting Persons of All Ages and Countries"

## Chapter 2: Who Strikes It Rich in a Gold Rush?

When I found myself in the terrifying and tenuous position of having to restart my financial life from scratch, I had what can only be described as a very faint glimmer of hope in the form of the internet. I told you about that glimmer in the first chapter of this book, and I really must emphasize to you that this was truly nothing but the faintest of lights in the darkness. I did not actually *know* how to make the internet work for me. All I knew was that I felt like it should be possible.

One reason I believed I ought to be able to quickly find an alternative to my old career that came with the same or better financial advantages was my acquaintance with a guy (spoiler alert: not me this time, although he is a good friend today) who lost everything he owned thanks to a fluke legal problem. Let's just say he owned quite a bit, and he made that fortune online to begin with. After he lost it all – and I do mean everything – he had to start over from ground zero. Do you know what happened?

**He became a millionaire again, even faster than the first time.**

I knew accelerated financial wealth and security was possible because I had watched him do it, and I also had seen plenty of companies experience incredible online success while I was still in the sales-and-marketing world. In fact, one of my clients was, at one point, America Online (that's AOL, if you are old enough to remember), back when they were the 800-pound gorilla in the online world. So, I had seen quick financial success happen on every point on the spectrum from the individual level to the mega-corporate level. What I had not seen at that point was the inner workings, the behind-the-scenes mechanics, that made that success possible.

In search of these mechanics, I asked myself a critically important question:

## In a gold rush, who makes the most money?

I'll give you a hint: it's not the miners – at least, not for the most part. Sure, a few of them may strike gold and become super-wealthy, but for every miner who strikes gold, there are thousands or tens of thousands who completely strike out and never make any money at all. There are many who gamble everything to join the gold rush and lose everything they have. So, it's not the miners.

But who does make the money in a gold rush?

There is one party who pretty much always ends up making money in a gold rush, and that person is the one who is selling the product or service that the people all rushing in a fever to the same place with the same goal – to find gold – need. That's right: it is the person selling the pickaxes. You have probably heard this concept presented in a lighthearted way, but it is nothing but cold, hard fact.

In the California Gold Rush back in the mid-1880s, more than 300,000 people mobbed the west in hopes of finding their fortunes. Do you know the names of the people who struck it rich and are known to this day thanks to the motherloads of gold they discovered? Nope. You do not. But there are some names we do know: the names of people who asked themselves a very important question about what they wanted to do while they were in California. That question was, "**What will the miners need in California?**"

The answer was the miners would need a lot of things! They needed tools like picks, shovels, and pans. They needed good, sturdy clothes to wear while digging, mining, and panning for gold. They needed a safe place to keep their money and, yes, their gold if they should find any. These individuals and, in some cases, businesses, decided to provide those resources to the miners, and you probably recognize their names to this day. Here are a few of them:

## Levi Strauss

Levi Strauss made his fortune providing sturdy clothes to miners. In fact, his jeans are ubiquitous even today. You almost certainly wear Levi jeans or know someone in your family who does so.

## Samuel Brannon

Samuel Brannon published a newspaper that he used to aggressively publicize the gold rush. He also, as it happened, owned the only store between San Francisco and the gold fields. In that store, he sold pans for $15 each. The miners bought those pans which, by the way, Brannon purchased at wholesale for 20 cents apiece. In just nine weeks, he made about $36,000, more than $5 million in today's money.

## Wells Fargo

Even if you did not recognize Levi Strauss or Samuel Brannon, I'm sure you recognize the name "Wells Fargo." They have made some business blunders in recent years, but even so, they retain nearly $2 trillion in assets on deposit and brought in more than $21 billion in cash the first quarter of 2019 alone. Where did Wells Fargo get started? Yep: the gold rush. They provided bank services to the miners, whether those miners were among the lucky few who made their fortune or the unlucky thousands who failed to do so. Pretty much all of them needed banking services one way or another, and Wells Fargo was there to provide those services.

During the California Gold Rush, you didn't want to be a gold miner. You wanted to be a Levi Strauss, a Samuel Brannon, or a Wells Fargo. You wanted to be the person selling the miners something they had to have in order to have any chance of success finding gold because then you would have a *guaranteed chance* of getting paid – and paid a lot.

## The Internet is a Literal Gold Mine

In today's world, the gold is not in the river or in the ground. The gold is on the internet. Do not be a person "digging around" on the internet hoping to turn up some gold.

**Be a person selling what the "miners" of today need: information, software, and tools.**

Today's internet miners, both successful and unsuccessful, need **information** so they can:

- Create products
- Launch those products
- Design effective sales funnels
- Create recurring revenue
- Start internet-based businesses
- Handle on- and offline marketing, including social media marketing, affiliate marketing, and content marketing
- Create effective hashtags

Today's internet miners, both successful and unsuccessful, need **software** to handle all the logistical angles of the things they created using the information they have found online. For example, they need website support, infrastructure for their email lists, and a program, product, or service to help them create effective follow-up campaigns.

Today's internet marketers, both successful and unsuccessful, need **tools** to help them use the software that is handling all the logistics associated with the things they have created. This might mean they need computers, for example, but more to the point it means they need today's online version of the pickaxe: lead generation systems, lead magnets, and the latest information and strategies for leveraging that traffic and creating income from it.

So, what does all of this mean to you? You're not a software designer, most likely. Do you have extensive experience in traffic generation, then? Do you coach others in creating recurring revenue? Well, you might, but probably not. Before you get too discouraged, however, think back to Samuel Brannon. He was not the maker of the $15 pan. He did not personally forge those picks and shovels. He just sold the products to the people who wanted them – at a huge markup! That is what you must do online, today.

## The Great Thing About the Internet Gold Rush

The internet gold rush is much, much bigger than the California Gold Rush. Even better, the miners online have a much better chance of being successful. This means that even more people need the information, software, and tools that every internet-based business and most non-internet-based businesses alike need in order to survive and have any chance of thriving. Furthermore, as more and more people succeed online, more and more people will mob the internet looking to strike it rich. If you are selling the pickaxes, you will always be in demand.

"But wait, I still am not a software designer, internet strategy expert, or extreme traffic generation guru," you are probably thinking right now. Well, I have some great news for you:

**The system is all ready and set up for you. All you have to do is start selling the pickaxes.**

What are today's pickaxes? Lead magnets, of course!

A lead magnet is an incentive that marketers offer

**Lead Magnet:** an incentive that marketers offer to potential buyers in exchange for their email address or other content, like a free PDF checklist, a report, an ebook, or a

to potential buyers in exchange for their email

address or other contact information, typically a piece of digital, content like a free PDF checklist, a report, an ebook, a whitepaper, a video, etc. These items tend to be relatively inexpensive to produce, much like Brannon's pans he purchased for a mere 20 cents each, but are extremely valuable to internet marketers, who will pay top dollar for effective tools that get the job done. Like Brannon, you can buy low and sell high, but you will just be buying the license to lead magnets and upsells rather than inexpensive pans.

How do you know what type of pickaxe internet marketers need *en masse*? That is one of the core principles of the Newtonian System, and is something we will explore in detail in the next chapter.

**"Truth is ever to be found in simplicity, and not in the multiplicity and confusion of things."**

Sir Isaac Newton

## Chapter 3: The Magic Ratio

When I was going through the ordeal that eventually led me to this point, I learned quickly that there are some things that internet businesses truly need and that the business owner will pay good money for, and some things that are sort of optional that may or may not attract the kind of transactional volume you are looking for when you get into the business of online marketing products and services.

At the time, I knew a lot of internet marketers. Almost all of them had an email list and were making about a dollar per email subscriber each month, at least. Now, even a relatively small list of a few hundred or a few thousand subscribers is incredibly valuable at a rate like that. But my friends often had tens or even hundreds of thousands of people on their email lists. You do the math!

I knew enough about internet marketing to know

**Opt-In List:** a list of emails from individuals who have specifically opted in to receive electronic correspondence from you.

**EPC:** earnings per click, calculated by dividing net earnings by total clicks.

that building up an *opt-in list* of subscribers clearly enabled people to have and control their own sources of income. Imagine having the power to click a button and send an email to your very own list of email subscribers. Imagine watching, in real time, as dozens, or hundreds, or even thousands of people visit a website, make purchases, and put cold, hard, cash in your pocket. *That is the promise of internet marketing.*

You see, email marketing is the real push-button traffic method. Willie Crawford, who, since 1996, has taught thousands of people to build successful online businesses, once said, "In the niches that I operate, I earn an average between $1 and $3 per month for every subscriber on my list." That, friends, is the true philosopher's stone: For every "base metal" individual engaged in their own business on the internet, you can create your own recurring gold rush by providing them with the things they need in order to succeed themselves. I think Isaac Newton himself would agree that the potential for generating wealth under those circumstances is nearly boundless, just as it would have been if he had discovered a real philosopher's stone.

## EPC 101

We have spent a lot of time talking about Isaac

Newton who, among many other things, was essentially the inventor of calculus. When I tell people that, and then I start talking about EPC, they tend to get a little nervous. They think I'm going to make them do some sort of crazy, difficult math to start making money online. Do not worry! EPC is a simple concept that you need to understand in order to calculate what type of returns your "pickaxes" will generate for you.

EPC stands for **Earnings Per Click**. You calculate EPC by dividing your net earnings by total clicks, so it is an equation, but a simple one. For example, say you are selling a product for $100. Don't have a product? Don't stress. You do not need one. We will deal with that next. For now, however, let's work on EPC.

If you have a product that sells for $100 and provides you with a net commission of $50, that means that for every product you sell, you *net* $50. For the purposes of this example, let's assume you sent an email to your email list and generated 1,000 clicks to the sales page of the product. Now, let's assume you make 25 sales, which results in *gross* sales of $2,500 and *net* sales to you of $1,250. Divide 1,250 by 1,000, and your EPC comes to $1.25.

Your EPC number is the key to your freedom and, more importantly, it is imminently achievable. An

EPC of $1.25 is not something you must wait and work for years to finally achieve. It is something you can accomplish *quickly* and *repeatedly* with the right principles in place. That is why I call it a "Magic Ratio," though it is not magic at all, but hard science!

## Opening the Window of Opportunity

In nearly everyone's life, there are a few windows of opportunity. These windows do not remain in your life forever, but while they are present, they mean the difference between struggling through life and, say, running into your first million dollars online – or, maybe, your second or third million. The millions are not the point here.

The point is that when the window of opportunity presents itself, you must act and *open it*. Far too many people allow those windows of opportunity to pass them by, leaving them behind forever. Even though they knew the window was there, they failed to open it. Action is the great restorer. Action is the builder of confidence. Inaction, on the other hand, is the destroyer. Inaction is both the cause and the result of fear.

"But what if I fail?" you may be thinking.

Well, you might. Most people fail at things from time to time. However, if you do not take any action, you may be quite confident you will fail *all of the time* rather than experiencing some setbacks but also massive success. Perhaps the action you take will be successful, but then you will have to adjust and refine your process; perhaps your action will not be successful, and you will have to revisit your strategy.

Even if your initial action accomplishes nothing, you will find that any action is better than none at all. You might expect an initial failure to stall you and discourage you, but you will find that the contrary is true. This is what successful people tend to refer to as "failing forward." It means what it sounds like it means: that even an action that is not immediately successful tends to create more positive momentum than doing nothing at all.

When I had my second heart attack. I had no choice but to act. If I failed, I would eventually die, or my family would eventually be in very dire straits because I was unable to support them. I had to jump in with both feet and, I will admit, I was terrified. However, what surprised me when I did jump in was that even when things did not go perfectly, I was able to course-correct with increasingly good results. I made positive steps forward even when I "failed," and that meant that I was able to start building a brand-new email list, from scratch, and get back on my feet again nearly immediately.

## You are Not Working Alone

One of the most important things to remember in conjunction with really understanding this crucial concept of failing forward is that this is not a myth. Internet marketing success is not the philosopher's stone. It is not something that we are seeking and hoping we will someday find. At this very minute, internet marketing is working *right now* for me and many, many others just like me. Soon, it will be working for you, and you will be using many of the very same tools I use. Now, does that mean everyone you ever sell a product will eventually become an internet millionaire? Of course not. It would be great if that were the case, but it is not. However, there will be lots of people who successfully support their businesses because of you and what you provide, and *you* can dramatically change your own circumstances for the better in the process.

You are not alone in the internet marketing space, and that is a good thing. I'm here with you, and so are many other incredibly successful individuals who, in some cases, make my own internet marketing success, which is by no means meager, look positively minor.

For example, one guy in our space recently reported that over the course of two years, starting from zero, he worked out a system that enabled him to make $1.1 million in a single year. Notice I said he started from zero. He is not some celebrity who already has a huge following and had an existing email list. He *started from zero*. Then, after the $1.1 million year, he more than doubled those numbers. The next year, he made $2.4 million in sales. How did he do this? Was he so brilliant that he created a brand-new system for making money online? No. He simply decided to take action and then kept on doing so until he hit that magic ratio. Once he found his own magic ratio, he just kept right on replicating and refining the process.

Those numbers in the example I just gave you are real numbers. They are not hypotheticals about what could happen if the stars align. They are not speculation about what you might achieve if you strike it lucky and manage to make your own personal philosopher's stone. They are real numbers that are wholly predictable and entirely replicable. They are numbers generated by someone smart enough to act while the window of opportunity was open and apply an existing system in his own life.

## A Question You Must Ask Yourself Before Reading Further

Ask yourself this question right now before you read any further:

**What did last year look like for you?**

Was it a good year? Why?

Was it an average year? Why?

Was it a desperate, awful, painful year? Why?

I realize that unless the answer is, "Yep, it was an awesome year!" you may not really want to take a close look at last year. However, it is very important you do so. You cannot identify and then leverage windows of opportunity if your eyes are closed; you have to remove the scales if you want to truly see. So take a hard look at last year, and then answer the question out loud. **"Last year was…for me, and here is why."** Say why.

Go ahead. Say it out loud. The whole thing.

Now, read on.

No matter how great or how painful last year was, this year can be a whole lot better. There is a window of opportunity now that will not last forever, but right now, I truly do not believe there has ever been a better opportunity to take this leap. In fact, I recently ran a search on Amazon about internet marketing and online marketing. When I searched the term "internet marketing" under books, there were a whopping 20,000 results. They were real results, not just things the algorithm threw up there to keep me happy. It was amazing. When I took my search to Google, the results were even more astounding: about 3 billion pages of results for the term. *There is so much interest in this topic.*

More importantly, the people who are interested in this term are people who act. When they search for things related to this term, they tend to make purchases in the wake of that search. You are in a position to sell pickaxes to internet marketers who want to buy, understand the concept of investing in their company, and are willing to buy repeatedly in order to refine their own processes. You must be willing to sell those pickaxes, refine your sales process, and then repeat it. If you can do this, if you are willing to take that action, then your window of opportunity is here. Don't be afraid to open it.

## "To every action, there is always opposed an equal reaction."

Sir Isaac Newton

## Chapter 4: Those Who Can, Teach

You have probably heard that obnoxious saying, "Those who can't do, teach." Well, offensive and wildly inaccurate nature of that statement aside – at least in business – I have to tell you that it is time to throw that statement and that mindset out. With all the interest in internet marketing, the people doing the teaching are the ones who *can* do, not the ones who cannot.

There are a lot of highly credible, extremely successful individuals out there getting very, very rich by teaching people about internet marketing concepts and how to implement internet marketing strategies to make money online. There is evidence everywhere of this. With every television show you watch, you see Twitter handles and other social media information being shared so you can follow not just the show, but also to hear insider jokes from the cast or receive updates when the show is not on. That is how we communicate today: online and all the time.

Do not forget, there are a growing number of millionaires out there thanks to internet marketing because the industry is, for now, nearly boundless.

Let's take a look at Mark Zuckerberg, founder and CEO of Facebook. It used to be that I did not particularly care to talk about Mark Zuckerberg because I found that people would sort of tune out when he came up. I'm telling you right now: do not tune out! Sure, Mark Zuckerberg is insanely wealthy. For most people, his wealth is far, far beyond their comprehension. Sometimes, I think his wealth is beyond his own comprehension. However, that does not mean that his wealth, his success, and, most importantly, his business, is irrelevant to you. In fact, it is highly, highly relevant, and the money you make from your internet business will spend exactly the same way Zuckerberg's will. The point is that there is an opportunity out there, and you must take it.

Sadly, Mark Zuckerberg, specifically, seems far more interested in keeping as much of his strategies and online activities secret (while looking uncomfortably closely at ours!) rather than sharing them with the world. Fortunately, there are lots and lots of successful internet marketers and internet business owners out there for us to examine who are not so furtive in their business dealings. There are people like me and people like my friend I mentioned in the previous chapter, who are perfectly delighted to not only prove they have created successful online businesses that generate reliable, high-volume, recurring income, but who are willing to help you gain access to the same systems they used.

Why would I, or anyone else, be willing to do this? Well, as I said, because this industry is, at present, wide open. People everywhere are fascinated with this topic, and successful instructors are able to amplify their income by teaching others how it works.

## The $2.1 Million Formula

If you are reading this book in digital format, I want you to set the e-reader down for just a moment and go get a pencil and a piece of paper. If you are reading it in hard copy, then feel free to make notes in the margin here. Just like Newton, you are probably going to want to do a little "figuring" during this part, and I want to make sure you have the materials you need right on hand because we

### The $2.1 Million Formula *or* The 3X Formula

A formula used repeatedly to generate large amounts of income at a predictable and accelerated rate.

X1: Subscribers

X2: Clicks

X3: EPC

are back to doing some of those Newtonian calculations I referred to earlier. You have the Magic Ratio, so now, it's time for the $2.1 million formula.

The $2.1 million formula is a formula that has been used repeatedly to generate large amounts of income. I originally named it the $2.1 million formula because it is a process that can generate $2.1 million in a single year, although people have used it to generate far more than that. In fact, one year, a colleague of mine made $14 million in one year with this formula. Some people refer to it as my Three-X (XXX) Formula now instead because they have made so much more money with it than the name suggests.

Those X's are the formula, so it is pretty simple. The first X stands for subscribers, the second X stands for clicks, and the third X stands for EPC. You already know what EPC is from our Magic Ratio chapter. Now, we will tackle the first X, subscribers. Those subscribers are the key to generating that income and creating your first $2.1 million (or more).

## 5 Steps to the Million-Dollar Email (Subscriber List)

The first step is getting those subscribers into an email list where you can email them, thereby putting them in a position to *click* (the second X, remember?). The first thing anyone starting this process must do in order to start reaching subscribers is to **register a domain name.**

A domain name is the name of a website. It is not
necessarily your company's name, though for many
websites the company name and the website are
the same, such as Facebook.com or Google.com.
However, you can register any domain name you
want as long as it is available, which means that no
one else has already paid for the right to use it.

To register your domain name, go to a domain
registrar like NameCheap.com that is relatively
inexpensive and popular with internet marketers.
Select your domain name, pay for it, and then
move on to the next step.

Second, you must purchase a **hosting account.**
Web hosting is, at its most basic level, an account
that gives you access to servers that store the files
and information you need to make a website. The
servers connect to the internet and make it
accessible to users. There are many options out
there for internet marketers seeking hosting
accounts. You do not need anything complicated,
however, so your best option is probably
HostGator. I started out with this service and use it
today. Invest in the simplest, cheapest package

Insider Insight: Autoresponders
There are many good autoresponder services out
there, but I definitely prefer GetResponse for three
primary reasons:

* It is very easy to use
* GetResponse will give you a completely free trial
to try it out
* There is a very good split-testing feature included

they offer, and that will fit your purposes perfectly.

Third, you will need to purchase access to an
**autoresponder.** Autoresponders are computer
programs that automatically answer emails. Like
hosting providers, there are many autoresponder
services that offer a variety of services, from the

very simple to the very complex. You need the autoresponder so you can assemble all your email subscribers in one place and then email them whenever you want.

To summarize where we are in the Million-Dollar Email Formula, which is part of the 3X Formula, let's review:

You now should have a **domain name,** a **hosting service** for that website, and an **autoresponder** to email your subscribers and consolidate them in one place. You are well on your way to writing and sending that million-dollar email now! So, let's continue.

Fourth, you must set up your **lead magnet**. Many people believe they do not know what a lead magnet is, but the truth is that nearly everyone has interacted with lead magnets before, and most of us do so on a daily basis! If you have ever been offered a special report, video, or PDF download in exchange for your email address or other information, then you have been offered a lead magnet. If you provided the requisite information to get that report, then you became a *lead* in the person's system who offered you the lead magnet. It literally attracted you into that person's email list, just like a magnet attracts iron. You became an *email subscriber* (remember that from earlier?) and now they can send you emails and, they hope, you will click on the links inside and then make purchases, creating a better EPC for that internet marketer.

One thing that you should do when you set up *your* lead magnet that nearly all internet marketers fail to do is incorporate a **lead magnet upsell**. That is the fifth thing you must do in the Million-Dollar Email formula. Failure to do so is an incredible error. You should always have an upsell set up so that after your lead magnet works and the potential lead becomes an actual lead, you have something to sell that lead immediately. Here is an example of how that might work:

Potential Lead Bobby *goes to your website and enters his name and email address. Now, Potential Lead Bobby is* Subscriber Bobby. *When Subscriber Bobby clicks the button to submit his information, instead of just a thank-you page, he sees a page that allows him to make a purchase from you. When Subscriber Bobby sees the page and makes a purchase, he is still a subscriber and now he is also* **Buyer Bobby**. *You have firmed up your relationship with Buyer Bobby and generated money on the front end of the relationship as well. That is incredibly valuable.*

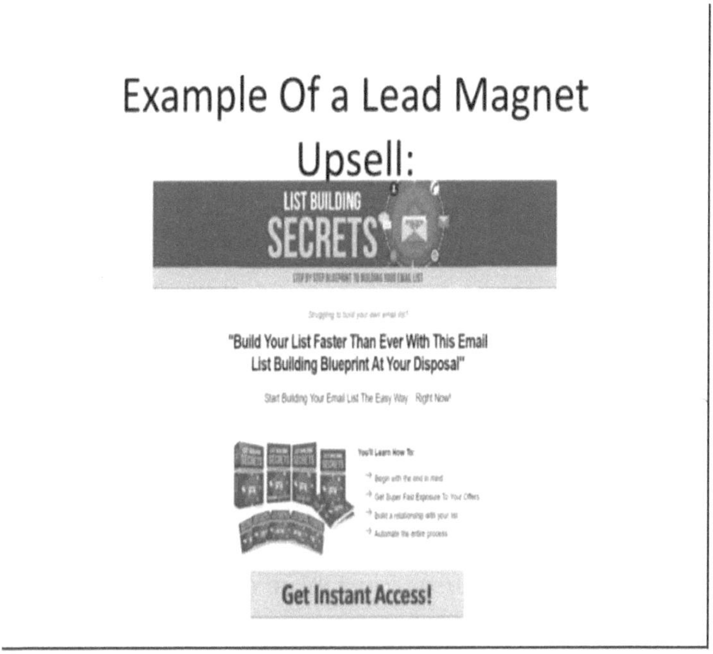

Figure 5. Example of an upsell page.

Now you have everything you need in order to generate your subscriber list, which you may also call an email list. As people encounter your lead magnet, they provide you with their email addresses and, in some cases, they go ahead and purchase your lead magnet upsell. Either way, they are now part of your subscriber database, and you can email them any time you want so that you can start generating more money.

Those five steps will take you to the position from which you can send that "million-dollar" email that changes everything for you. Those subscribers are the first X. Once you have everything in place to gain subscribers, it is time to optimize the components of your second X, your clicks or your traffic.

## 2 Essential Components to Optimize the Second X

Now that you have an infrastructure to support your subscribers, it is time to start sending more of them into your system. This means you need more traffic, and traffic is part of the second X in the 3X equation because to get more *clicks*, you need more traffic.

I'm going to tell you a little story about when I first got started with the 3X Formula. First off, I have to emphasize to you that the feeling you get when this process starts to work is like nothing you have felt before. It is just so uplifting. The first time you realize Potential Lead Bobby has now become 50 or 100 Potential Lead Bobby's and now they are all Subscriber Bobby's and Buyer Bobby's *and there is money in your mailbox and your bank account thanks to their purchases*, it is like the sun coming out after the darkest storm.

You start to feel such motivation and positivity that you just cannot wait to refine your system. You want to look at your clicks. You cannot wait to evaluate emails. You start testing new types of subject lines and offers to see what works best. It is thrilling, and it is one of the best times in your business because, as you may remember, I told you that action creates more action. If you have possibly been less than active in the past and now you can feel the energy just speeding through you, you will feel like you are unstoppable.

Feeling unstoppable is a wonderful, powerful feeling, and the best way to optimize your results while you are feeling motivated and invincible is to make sure the following two components in your system are the absolute best fit for your business:

1. **Your lead magnet**
2. **Your lead magnet upsells**

Think about it: your lead magnet is the page and the offer on it that converts Potential Lead Bobby to Subscriber Bobby. It is the essential first step in your system because if Subscriber Bobby never exists, then you have no one to ever see your lead upsells and become buyers and, ultimately, you still have no income flowing in. Your lead magnet has two components: the offer and the webpage upon which it sits.

We will deal with how to optimize both of these in just a moment after addressing your upsells. Why are those so important? Well, for starters, those upsells are the first opportunity you have to generate income from your relationship with Subscriber Bobby. You put a lot of work into this guy, and so far, he has taken your free offer, your lead magnet, and not paid you back in income. That is okay, but you want to change that. Lead magnet upsells are your first opportunity to do so. Secondly, when Subscriber Bobby becomes Buyer Bobby, he is immediately in a more "committed" relationship with you. Once someone buys something from you, even if it is something small, they are far more likely to do so again. You want as many subscribers converting to buyers as early as possible in the process so that they are in the "habit" of buying from you as early as possible.

## Lead Magnet Optimization

We touched on lead magnets already, but I want to talk in this section about how to make sure your lead magnet is the most compelling offer possible. I find that the best lead magnets tend to be free reports, and they should even have a magic number: 7. For example, a free report titled, "7 Steps to Total Market Domination" would likely be a good offer, but there are also things that can make it better. For example, "Market Domination" might be too generic. Maybe you should use "Real Estate Market Domination" or "Stock Market

Domination" or "Internet Marketing Domination"
or even "Niche Marketing Domination."

All of those sound great. They look great. *But are
they great?* The only way to find out is to split test
them to figure out which one works the best. It will
probably not be the one you expect – at least not
at first, so do not be disappointed when you guess
wrong. The important thing is to trust the process,
because if you ignore the indicators that tell you
which lead magnet or which web page is the best
for your purposes, you will either make *less money*
or you will make *zero money.*

Split testing, which is also called A/B testing, makes
me think of an eye exam. You sit in the chair and
the ophthalmologist says, "Is number 1 or number
2 better?" and flips the lens. You answer number 1.
Then, they say, "Is number 1 or number 3 better?"
and you swear they are the same two lenses, but
you are not really sure, and you answer number 3.
Then, they say, "Okay, number 3, or number 4?"
and the process continues until the doctor feels
confident they know your prescription. That is split
testing, and the same basic process applies to both
your lead magnet in terms of what it is (a report, a
PDF, an ebook, etc.), what it is titled, and where it
is presented (your website). When you have the
combination of the best lead magnet presented in
the best light on the best webpage for you, then

you have positioned yourself to fire up the $2.1

> **Split Testing:** also called A/B testing, is the process of comparing multiple versions of the variant to statistically determine which one is more effective.

> **Radical Variant:** also called a radical variation, used in split testing to determine if something vastly different from the initial variant would be more effective.

Million Formula, write the Million-Dollar (or more) emails, and really start watching Newtonian Wealth Generation at its finest.

To split test, do exactly what the ophthalmologist does, except with your webpages and your lead magnets. We will talk about the webpages first. Once you have a website ready, start tracking how well it works. Say, for example, your first try converts at about 30 percent, meaning that for every 100 people that visit, 30 people sign up to get your lead magnet and become subscribers. That is a 30 percent opt-in rate. That 30 percent is, well, average. You can easily beat your competition simply by split testing.

Once you have your first page, then you design another one. It can be similar to the first or it can be a radically different design, what is called a "radical variation." This means it is very, very different from the original. If your original is very sleek and professional, then your radical may be plain, simple text with very little formatting. It could be downright ugly.

Now you have two webpages, and you track your conversions for both. Some internet marketers will split test three pages at a time, keeping the original, refining the original, and adding in a radical variation. Let's say you do this and the original keeps converting at 30 percent, the improved original converts at 19 percent, and the radical variation converts at 49 percent. Well, that tells you the radical variation is the keeper. Now, you can keep improving it, but you know it is the best of the three you have.

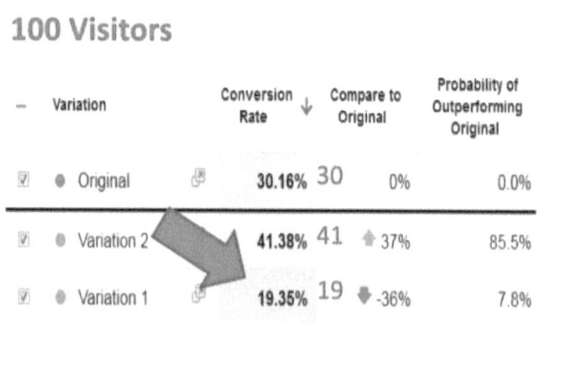

## 100 Visitors

| — Variation | | Conversion Rate ↓ | | Compare to Original | Probability of Outperforming Original |
|---|---|---|---|---|---|
| ☑ ● Original | 🔗 | 30.16% | 30 | 0% | 0.0% |
| ☑ ● Variation 2 | | 41.38% | 41 ⬆ 37% | | 85.5% |
| ☑ ● Variation 1 | 🔗 | 19.35% | 19 ⬇ -36% | | 7.8% |

*Figure 6. Sample of a split test.*

Making that type of jump is the difference between being successful and being wildly successful. Once you have selected the primary design, then you can change the headlines, the title of the report, etc.; compare the effectiveness of all of your changes; and keep improving your conversion rate. Once you have your webpage optimized and the best lead magnet in place, then you are ready to do the same thing with your lead magnet upsells.

Always keep refining, testing, and improving. Never assume your gut knows best. Always track, test, and improve your lead magnet and lead magnet upsells so your *cash flow* will be optimized as well.

**"The proper method for inquiring after the properties of things is to deduce them from experiments."**

Sir Isaac Newton

## Chapter 5: Scientifically Establishing Your Email Profit Center for Permanent Newtonian Profits

Now that you have the infrastructure in place to bring in leads, convert them to subscribers, and then convert them to buyers, it is time to focus in on the real profit center in your Newtonian System for Lasting & Accelerated Financial Wealth and Security: **the email.**

At this point, nearly everything you do is going to be about the emails you are sending to your subscribers. Remember, subscribers are the leads that you converted and who now have opted in and expect to hear from you regularly. Some of your subscribers will also already be your buyers; others will still be on the fence about buying but have clearly demonstrated they want to hear from you because *they gave you their email address for that purpose!*

So, let's email them, but you have to do it right. Emailing the right way means writing the best emails possible to get your audience to react the way that you want. More importantly, however, emailing the right way means writing the best **subject lines** so that people will open your emails in the first place. Fail to get those opens, and the best lead magnets, the best upsells, the best everything is worth very, very little because no one is actually seeing any of it.

In my journey as an internet marketer, the "big money" and the real financial freedom in internet marketing is found in your ability to either write, craft, buy, or at least recognize the very best emails and subject lines.

**The better the subject lines, the more opens you get.**

**The better the email, the more opens convert to clicks.**

**The more conversions to clicks, the more opportunities to convert to sales, and so on. I imagine you get the picture.**

So, how do you create a good email subject line and good email content?

# How Much Money Do You Really Want to Make?

Before you read any farther, I want you to do something for me. Drop your pen or pencil. Put down your notepad and notes. Close your eyes and lean back. Clear your mind.

**Now, decide how much money you want to make.**

Once you have that number, do not get distracted. I am not asking you to tell me (or yourself) what you would do with the money. I just need you to answer:

**How much money do you need?**

Think about what you would do if money were not an object. Now, think about how much money you would need for money not to be an object. That number is how much money you need to make. Convert that number from dollars to clicks, and you have the answer to your money problems, whatever they are, on whatever scale, literally written right in front of you.

You know it: split testing. Just as you did with the

webpages and the lead magnets, when it comes to split testing your emails, you start with one piece of the puzzle and then start solving and evolving. For example, say you have an offer that is making about $1 per click, which means that every single click you get in your email, you are making one dollar. One more click equals one more dollar. Often, the correlation really is that direct. So, you need to get your hands on proven emails and subject lines that will get you more clicks and, by extension, more dollars. Now, you should take a look at the sidebar to the right. It will help you moving forward to have your own personal money number in your mind.

## The Only 2 Methods You Need to Know to Make All the Money You Want from Your Email List

Once you have taken a look at the sidebar to the right, we will walk through the process for you. Let's say for the moment you wanted $100 a day in order to have enough money. That equates to $3,000 a month, or $36,000 a year. It also equates to 100 clicks a day, which is not that hard to do. In fact, doing double that occurs routinely in internet marketing businesses that are operating just barely on average.

Of course, a lot of people want to make a lot more than $100 a day. They want $500 a day or $1,000 a day. It starts to feel like a great deal of money, but when you think of it in clicks, you have the metric you need to meet in order to make those values happen.

$500 a day? 500 clicks a day. 15,000 clicks a month.

$1,000 a day? 1,000 clicks a day. 30,000 clicks a month.

The numbers may seem big, but they are solid numbers you can aim for and clearly see how close you are getting. That is very important if you are going to make split-testing work for you.

## Affiliate Offers

So, now that you know what kind of click numbers you are aiming for, it is time to start refining your sales process. That means you need to start mailing affiliate offers. An affiliate offer is an offer you make to your list from a third party. When someone buys that offer, then you receive an **affiliate commission.** You do not have to create a product, support the product, or deliver any products or services. In fact, all you have to do is get the right affiliate offers in front of your email list with the right email subject line and the right email copy. Then your list clicks and does the rest!

Most internet marketers get their start in affiliate marketing, although few remain there permanently. Affiliate marketing is one of the fastest and easiest ways to get started in the business. Successful affiliate marketers have a simple mantra:

*Find an offer. Mail an offer. Find an offer. Mail an offer.*

Affiliate marketing can feel a little bit like fishing because you are sending out offers to see what kind of "bites" you get from your list. When you email a product, take a minute to take note of what you mailed, how you mailed it, and what the response from your list was. Essentially, you are fishing for EPCs instead of bass or salmon. When you end up with an EPC of $2, say, and you are accustomed to $1, then you keep that $2 product in the rotation because if it sold that way once, it is likely to again.

So why does affiliate marketing work? Well, there are tens of thousands of companies out there that operate online businesses. They are doing a lot of hard work creating products, building the site, setting up the infrastructure, and operating free programs to enable you and anyone else who is eligible to become an affiliate. Once you are an affiliate, every time you sell one of their products, you will get an affiliate commission.

The key to successful affiliate marketing is knowing what offers are converting, what offers will appeal to your subscribers, and what affiliate marketing companies are best at helping you make money. You will soon discover the more active you are in this space, the more people will send you information about affiliate products in hopes that you will promote them. This may help you identify good affiliate products, but always be careful to ascertain where the numbers come from. I have seen affiliate products with EPC values in the triple digits, but not every high-dollar EPC has been calculated correctly. Affiliate marketers need you to promote them. Every click is another profit for them as well as you! Some will not hesitate to "blur the lines" if they think it will help them convince you to send out their emails.

## Track Your Results

As you start mailing out affiliate offers, track your
progress. Affiliate offers that garner good response
in terms of a high volume of responses or a high
return may be worth repeating. You can test, split
test, and track your affiliate program just as you
can test, split test, and track anything else – and
you should!

## Affiliate Marketing is Big Business

There are many affiliate marketing platforms out
there offering hundreds and even thousands of
affiliate products that you can easily access and
promote. Some of the most popular are:

- **Warrior Plus**
- **JVZoo**
- **ClickBank**

To give you an idea of how big this space is and the kind of potential there is in affiliate marketing for you, take a look at the numbers below. They are the cumulative revenues from these companies, meaning how much money their clients have made:

- Warrior Plus: **$53 million** (at present, it may be nearly double that, but this platform does not report regularly)
- JVZoo: **$50 million**
- ClickBank: **$2 billion**

## Joint Ventures and Other Offers

At the beginning of this chapter, I mentioned there are two types of email marketing strategies that encompass literally all you need to know to make all the money you want in email marketing. That is true. The first is certainly affiliate marketing, and that is particularly important to a new internet marketer because it is **simple** and **fast.**

However, as I noted toward the end of the affiliate marketing section, you will also find that it is highly profitable to create your own products in order to generate profits that you do not have to split with another party. Of course, there are some costs associated with this strategy since you must support your own products yourself rather than simply sending your buyers to another individual.

When internet and email marketers find themselves searching for higher returns than the EPCs conventionally available in affiliate products, they often find themselves attracted to joint ventures, or JVs. JVs are essentially affiliate marketing, but you work directly with the product provider and the promotions are more extensive. In most cases, the commissions are more extensive as well, which is one reason so many email marketers eventually graduate to this level despite massive success at the affiliate marketing level.

Email marketers often sell "drops" or "blasts" to their lists as well. I would give you a word of warning on this topic: Selling access to your list can hurt your list, so be wary of going overboard in this. It is far easier for a promoter to pay a flat fee to reach a high-caliber list like yours, use their own lead magnet to "scrape" the list of all your good leads, then promote their products later and not share anything with you. Conversely, you may occasionally wish to use this strategy yourself with email marketers who are willing to permit outside advertisers. This is deserving of an entire book unto itself, however, so that is all the mention we will make of it here.

## Chapter 6: Don't Be Afraid to be the "Flyer"

If you have a daughter who is involved in cheerleading, then you probably are familiar with the term, "flyer." If not, I'll take a quick moment to explain. The "flyer" in cheer is the girl who gets thrown into the air and then caught before she hits the ground. These girls may fly very high, and it can be scary – especially since they tend to be the smallest, youngest, and lightest on the squad. Being a "base" is often more attractive to the timid simply because the bases, as the name suggests, keep their feet firmly on the ground and support the rest of the team – literally on their backs or shoulders in a lot of cases.

Here's a little bit of science-meets-cheerleading observation that might startle you:

**Isaac Newton was a self-proclaimed flyer.**

Surprised? You shouldn't be. Okay, so Newton may not have been shouting "Go, Team!" and waving pompoms at every opportunity, but he viewed his own staggeringly enormous accomplishments through the lens of a true flyer. Of his discoveries, he said, "If I have seen further than others, it is by standing on the shoulders of giants."

Newton was not afraid to stand at the top of the pyramid, so to speak, and look forward with intense curiosity and creativity. He also was not ashamed to leverage the knowledge and experience of others in order to enhance his own learning and understanding of the world. Even more important, he did not view his reliance on that knowledge and support from his "bases" (his giants) as something to be hidden, but rather credit that should be given where it was due. Newton was the ultimate flyer, and he was rewarded with incredible insights and scientific understanding that arguably no one has surpassed in terms of volume or substance since.

**Be like Newton. Be a flyer.**

What do I mean by that? Well, a lot of internet marketers and email marketers feel like they have to reinvent the wheel every time they send an email. They spend a distressing amount of time trying to figure out new ways to do time-tested, proven, *profitable* activities and, in the process, they often end up losing the profitable side of those activities completely. As an instructor, it is incredibly frustrating to watch!

I am telling you: **Be like Isaac Newton. Be a proud flyer.**

Think about it. Do you disagree with any of the following statements?

- **"For every action, there is an equal and opposite reaction."**
- **"Force equals mass times acceleration."**
- **"Every object that is in a state of uniform motion will remain in that state of motion unless an external force acts on it."**

Even if you have not seen these in a while, you probably instinctively agreed with them. After all, they are Newton's three laws of motion, some of the most foundational science ever. Using these three laws, you can make all sorts of other discoveries, conduct lots of research, or just invent a machine that makes use of this information even if you do not understand why it is true or how Newton discovered it. In these scenarios, Newton is *your* giant, *your* base, and you are the flyer.

Now, let's think about the book you are nearly done reading. It is also full of straightforward, fundamental truths about how email marketing works. I wrote this book in this manner so that you did not have to deal with the *why* so much as the "how to leverage this information quickly and profitably" angle of email marketing because when I needed to get started in this business, I did not have time to spare. Most people these days do not.

**That is why I gave you systems, ratios, formulas, and methods to work with, not concepts, ideas, and brainstorming opportunities.**

Am I saying you should never be creative in business? Absolutely not! In fact, one of the best places to be creative is in the split-testing portion of your email marketing business. That is the perfect venue in which to indulge your gut, your imagination, your radical wild side and clearly see whether you might be on to something new and groundbreaking of your own.

But in the interim, let's get the business started. Let's get that money coming in. This is the Newtonian *System* for Accelerated, Lasting Financial Wealth and Security! It's a system for a reason, so let the system work for you. The time has come to act, to take what you need, so make this success, this security, this peace of mind and improved quality of life, happen. Make it happen now, and let's get started together.

"If I have seen further than others, it is by standing upon the shoulders of giants."

Sir Isaac Newton

*Greg Gootee spent nearly 30 years as an extremely successful marketing professional before retiring in 2003. He is now a full-time email marketer and online entrepreneur dedicated to helping motivated individuals attain ultimate freedom and transform their lives. Learn more about Greg's Newtonian System for Accelerated, Lasting Financial Wealth & Security at NewtonianSystem.com.*

www.ingramcontent.com/pod-product-compliance
Lightning Source LLC
Chambersburg PA
CBHW021907170526
45157CB00005B/2003